Death Zone:
Extreme Exploration

Written by Paul Harrison

Contents

Collins

1 Introduction

Why do we explore? Why do we need to know what lies over the horizon? In the beginning we did it because we had to – to find food or shelter, for example. Later we explored for the challenge. When the mountaineer George Mallory was asked why he wanted to climb Mount Everest, his reply was simply, "Because it's there."

However, our desire to explore sometimes comes at a price. Venturing into the unknown is difficult and dangerous. Sometimes explorers pay the ultimate price and never return. Yet we still push on to find out more, venturing into the most extreme and deadly environments: the highest mountains; the deepest seas; parched deserts; and even into space. These are the places that push us to our very limits – and beyond!

2 All around the world

Imagine what it must feel like travelling into the unknown. Although the ancient Greeks knew the earth was round, many, many people believed the world was flat. There was only one way to find out for sure – to sail around the world or fall off the edge trying.

Fame and fortune

The first expedition to try and sail all the way around the world was led by the Portuguese sailor Ferdinand Magellan. Even those people who believed the world was round thought he was mad to try and attempt it. If sea monsters didn't get him, then deadly killer fogs certainly would. His chances of surviving the journey were practically nil.

Nevertheless, in 1519 he set off from Spain with five ships and a crew of around 260 people. Although Magellan imagined the voyage would lead to fame and fortune, it did not turn out as he'd hoped.

Ferdinand Magellan

5

Magellan was not a popular leader. In the first winter, some of his crew rebelled and he had them executed. He also lost two ships. As they sailed across the Pacific, some of his crew starved to death and others got scurvy – a deadly disease caused by a lack of vitamins. Then, when Magellan arrived at the Philippines, he attacked a local tribe and was killed in the resulting battle. Magellan's voyage was over.

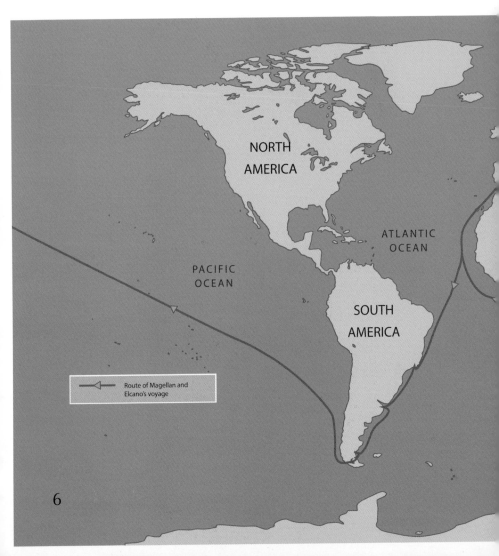

NORTH AMERICA

ATLANTIC OCEAN

PACIFIC OCEAN

SOUTH AMERICA

Route of Magellan and Elcano's voyage

The expedition continued though and, against all the odds, returned to Spain under the command of Juan Sebastian de Elcano. The expedition had proved that it was possible to sail all the way around the world. Success came at a terrible price, however – only one ship and 18 men survived the journey.

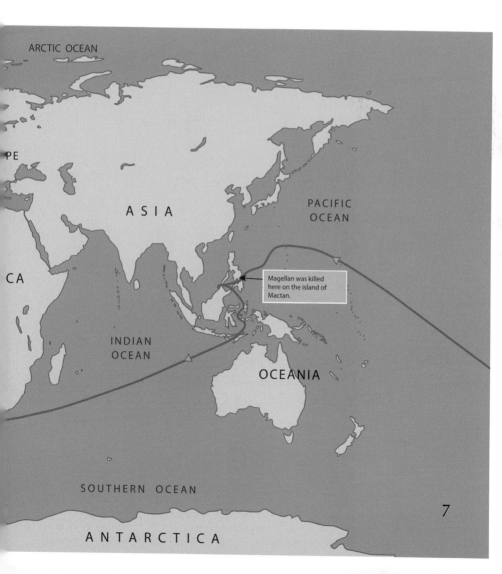

Magellan was killed here on the island of Mactan.

The impossible passage

Circumnavigating the world was dangerous, difficult and time-consuming. If a route over the top of North America linking the Atlantic and Pacific Oceans could be found, it would cut thousands of kilometres off the distance. The hunt for the so-called Northwest Passage was on – but at a cost no one imagined.

A R C T I C

O C E A N

Ellesmere

Axel
Heiberg
Island

Island

Greenland
(Denmark)

———— Northwest
Passage

Queen Elizabeth Islands

Parry Islands

Melville
Island

Baffin

Bay

BEAUFORT
SEA

Banks
Island

Devon Island

Prince
Albert
Peninsula

Prince of
Wales Island

Baffin
Island

Victoria
Island

Melville
Peninsula

C A N A D A

Frozen seas

The biggest problem with finding a northwest passage was the climate. The top of North America was in the Arctic Circle and was often very cold – so cold that the sea was frozen for a lot of the year. Even during the summer when there was less ice, there were the problems of poor weather, shallow waters and moving sand bars – which are like underwater sand dunes that reach close to the surface.

John Cabot

Did you know?
Italian explorer John Cabot led the first two expeditions to discover the Northwest Passage in 1497 and 1498. Neither he nor his crew survived the second attempt.

Terrible failure

There were many attempts to find the passage.
Perhaps the most famous was the expedition led by British
explorer Sir John Franklin. He set sail in 1845 with two
large, well-equipped ships, *HMS Erebus* and *HMS Terror*,
unaware of the disaster that would await them.

The ships got stuck in sea ice for a year and a half, and in 1847 Franklin and 23 others were dead. The survivors set out on foot to try and find help. They ended up starving to death on their journey. Some even tried eating each other in a desperate attempt to survive. Although many attempts were made to rescue the crews, no survivors were found.

Did you know?
The first person to find a route over the top of North America was the Swedish explorer Roald Amundsen in a voyage that lasted from 1903–1906.

He was also the first to reach the South Pole!

3 Down in the depths

While we now know a lot about the surface of our seas, the least explored part of our planet is actually what lies beneath the waves. As water covers around 70% of the earth's surface, that leaves a huge area we have yet to discover.

Challenging conditions

Imagine sitting for hours on end with your legs cramped up high near your chest, barely able to move, surrounded by scientific equipment, switches and dials. This is exactly what film director James Cameron had to do to reach the deepest point on Earth – Challenger Deep.

Challenger Deep is an underwater valley at the bottom of the Pacific Ocean. It lies 11,000 metres below the surface of the water at the southern end of the Mariana Trench. Conditions at this depth are unbearably harsh. There is no light as it's too deep for sunlight to reach the bottom, so it's pitch black. It's also very cold (around two degrees centigrade) and the weight of all the water above Challenger Deep would crush a normal submarine instantly. To reach such a place James Cameron needed a very special type of vehicle: a one-person submersible called Deepsea Challenger.

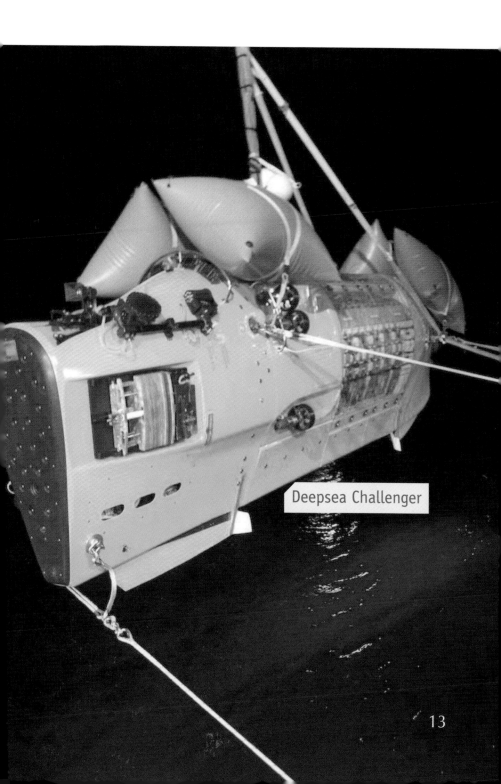

Deepsea Challenger

A light lunch

Remarkably, even at the great depths of Challenger
Deep, life thrives. From tiny creatures called microbes
to 30-centimetre-long shrimp-like animals, sea creatures
live in this harsh, pitch-black environment. Conditions are
too bad for plants to grow, so most creatures survive by
eating any dead animals that have sunk to the ocean floor.
Amazingly, some creatures at this depth can generate their
own light. This is called bioluminescence and is used to
attract unwary animals, which end up becoming lunch!

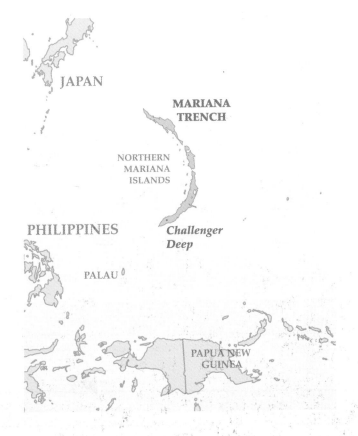

First sight

The first people to explore the deepest parts of the sea were William Beebe and Otis Barton in the early 1930s. Their craft was a round, metal ball called the Bathysphere. They travelled almost a kilometre below the surface off the coast of Bermuda and discovered completely new varieties of sea creature. Cameras in those days weren't good enough to take pictures in those conditions, so Beebe and Barton had to describe what they saw to artists afterwards.

Barton, Beebe and the Bathysphere

15

4 On top of the world

Challenger Deep is the lowest point on Earth, but the highest points also present a challenge to the adventurous. Mountains dominate a landscape, perilous places that will catch out the ill-prepared, the unwary or the plain unlucky. Each year, thousands of people attempt to climb the most famous mountains. For many, it's the last thing they do.

The death zone

The world's highest mountains pose an extra threat to the health of climbers. Humans need oxygen to breathe, but above 8,000 metres the levels of oxygen become dangerously low. This is what climbers call the death zone, and the longer you spend there the more dangerous it is. Here climbers can suffer headaches and dizziness, lung problems and the increased risk of deadly heart attacks or brain injuries.

The highest

When you climb Mount Everest, you are literally on the top of the world as this is the highest point on Earth. The mountain stands 8,848 metres tall and can be found in the Himalayan mountain range that spreads from Pakistan to China. In 1953, Tenzing Norgay and Sir Edmund Hillary became the first people to climb the mountain. It took six long difficult weeks to reach the summit.

Sir Edmund Hillary and Tenzing Norgay on Mount Everest

Deadliest climb

On one day alone, 11 climbers died attempting to climb Mount Everest, but Everest isn't the deadliest mountain. This unwanted title belongs to another Himalayan mountain called Annapurna I. Although it's only the tenth highest mountain in the area, for every three climbers that reach the summit, one will die trying.

Even successful climbers can suffer. Maurice Herzog and Louis Lachenal – the first people to climb Annapurna I – had to have all their toes chopped off because the extreme cold killed the flesh on their feet. Herzog lost all of his fingers too!

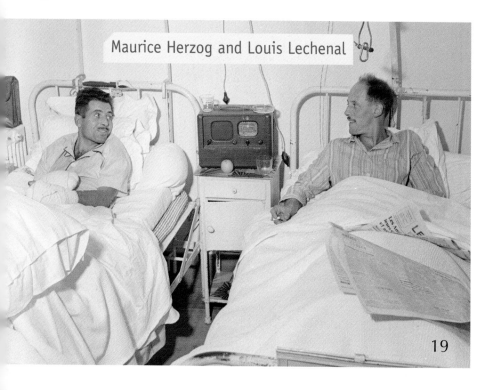

Maurice Herzog and Louis Lechenal

5 Going underground

For many people it's not exploring the surface of the earth that excites them – but what's underneath. Caves have always fascinated people. Our ancestors used them for shelter, we've stored precious objects in them during wars, and we've mined them for valuable ores and minerals.

It's no wonder people find them amazing – if dangerous – places to explore.

Grisly discovery

Historians exploring difficult to reach caves in north-eastern Scotland made a terrible discovery. They found lots of human bones, which were thousands of years old. Most belonged to people who had been buried there. However, they also found children's bones which, from the way the bones were damaged, suggested that the children had been sacrificed! Why the children met this grisly end, we'll never know.

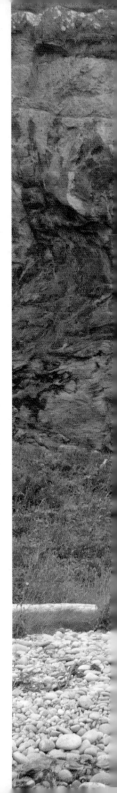

Did you know?
The study of caves is
called speleology.

Deadly rescue

On 23rd June 2018, a boy's football team went on a day trip to the Tham Luang caves in Thailand. While the 12 boys and their coach explored the ten-kilometre-long series of caves, heavy rain led to the caves suddenly flooding. The team were trapped four kilometres from the cave entrance. Without help they would all have died, either from starvation or by drowning. It was a race against time that needed hundreds of rescuers and a team of divers to succeed.

The team were taken out by the divers, who led them through the pitch-black water. It was risky as none of the boys had used diving equipment before – some of them couldn't even swim – and each journey took hours in the swirling floodwater.

The rescue took three days, but all the team were saved. Unfortunately, two of the divers were not so lucky and died as a result of the heroic plan.

6 River routes

Great civilisations have grown up on the banks of important rivers. Explorers travel great distances to discover where the world's mightiest rivers begin.

Illness and arguments

In the 1850s, British explorers Richard Burton and John Speke led an expedition to find the source of the River Nile, the world's longest river. They struggled through swamps, scrambled up mountains and were bitten all over by insects. Both Burton and Speke fell seriously ill but, while Burton stayed at camp, Speke pushed on and found the main source of the Nile at a place he called Lake Victoria. Burton refused to believe Speke had found the source and the pair returned to England as enemies. An expedition to the same area in 1875 would prove that Speke was right.

Richard Burton and John Speke

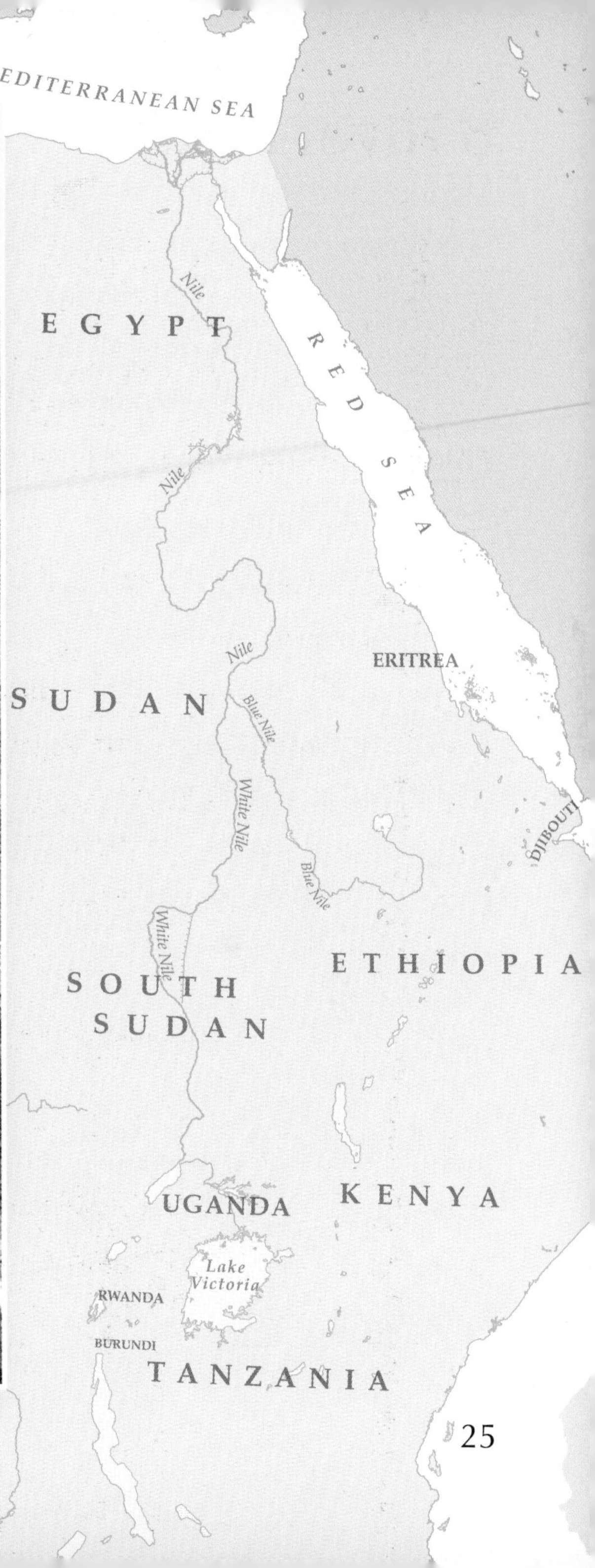

EGYPT

RED SEA

Nile

Nile

SUDAN

Nile

ERITREA

Blue Nile

White Nile

DJIBOUTI

Blue Nile

White Nile

SOUTH
SUDAN

ETHIOPIA

UGANDA

KENYA

Lake
Victoria

RWANDA

BURUNDI

TANZANIA

High-tech hunting

Modern-day explorers use more high-tech methods to find where rivers begin. Photographs taken by space satellites can show explorers where to look and the route that rivers take. This doesn't take away all the hard work and danger though – explorers still have to be there on the ground to check whether what the photographs seem to show is correct.

In 2013, James Contos and his team tried to find the source of the Amazon River, which snakes through Peru and Brazil in South America. Contos had to walk and kayak his way through the heat of the rainforest. At one point, he fell and lost his boat and equipment in the very river he was trying to study. That could have been a fatal error – the Amazon River is home to deadly fish called piranha, crocodile-like creatures called caiman, and many different diseases that are carried in water! It was worth the effort. They discovered that the Amazon was at least 75 kilometres longer than people had believed.

Did you know?
The Amazon might not be the longest river, but it is the largest river on earth. No other river carries as much water as the Amazon.

James Contos
by the Amazon River

27

7 Welcome to the jungle

Tropical rainforests, such as the one the Amazon River runs through, are hot, damp, dark and mysterious places. Scientists believe that half of all life on land can be found in rainforests. In a recent study of the Amazon rainforest in South America, scientists discovered on average two new species of animal a day! There is still much to be discovered in these amazing places.

Treasure hunters

Generally, explorers from Europe didn't go to the rainforests to look at the wildlife – they went to get rich and famous, no matter how this affected the local people or the area. One of the most famous of these was called Colonel Percy Fawcett. He believed there was a lost city full of treasure in the Brazilian rainforest. He called this city "Z", and in 1925 went off to find it. He and his team went into the forest and were never seen or heard from again. People went looking for them and at least 100 of these rescuers never returned either. The rainforest holds the secret of Percy Fawcett's fate!

Colonel Percy Fawcett

Lost forest

You might think it would be difficult for a rainforest to remain hidden, but that's exactly what happened in Mozambique in Africa. In 2012, a scientist called Julian Bayliss was studying satellite pictures of the country. He spotted a small rainforest on the top of an extinct volcano in Mozambique called Mount Lico. The forest was only the size of around 40 football pitches and, as the volcano was over 400 metres tall with very steep sides, hardly anyone had ever been there. It was difficult for the scientists to get to, but it meant that they had a chance to study a forest that was practically undisturbed – showing them what rainforests are like without the impact of human life.

Important places

Scientists believe rainforests are vital to our survival. Apart from the job the forests do in helping to control the earth's climate, the plants themselves are hugely important. They provide food, useful things like rubber, and are used in medicines. There are so many new plants to discover, so who knows what we might find and how we might benefit.

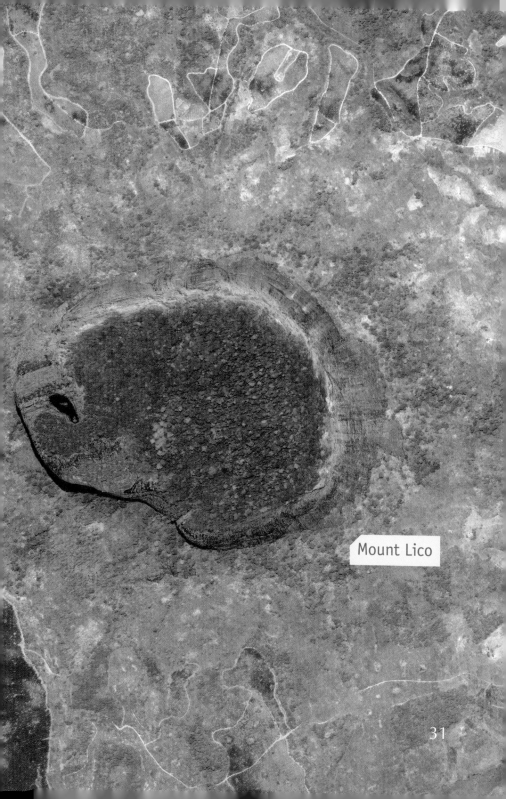

Mount Lico

Legends of the lost

Legends of ancient cities, long abandoned and now lost in history have always excited explorers. Were any of these cities real? More importantly, could any of them be found and what treasures were left to be discovered?

Honduran rainforest

The White City

There have long been tales of lost cities, deep in the rainforest of Honduras in Central America. In 2012, with the help of laser equipment called LIDAR, the rumours could be properly investigated. LIDAR can see objects hidden by forests or even underground. When LIDAR was used over the Honduran rainforest, the remains of a city were found, with great buildings, open spaces and pyramids. The rumours called it the White City. As historians travelling to the site discovered, science hadn't just unearthed a new city, they had found a lost civilisation. The identity of the people who built this magnificent city remains a mystery.

remains of the ancient White City

33

8 Secrets of the seas

How do you find something buried under the seabed –
especially if you don't know exactly where to look?
You rely on detective skills, hard work and a
slice of good fortune. A team of European
and Egyptian experts were exploring
the coast of Egypt, searching for the
lost city of Thonis-Heracleion.
After four years surveying the area,
they started using machines that
work like underwater vacuum
cleaners to remove the sand.
They were delighted at
what they found –
they had unearthed
the 2,700-year-old city!
The city had sunk into
the sea and been largely
forgotten; but here it was,
revealed again, for the first
time in over 1,000 years.

The head of a giant stone statue
of a pharaoh found close to the
great temple of Thonis-Heracleion

9 Shifting sands

The way a landscape changes over time presents a challenge for explorers. Deserts, which are constantly changing and altering are one of the harshest environments for explorers, with shifting sands, little water to drink and few plants to eat. In addition, they can be blisteringly hot during the day and freezing cold at night.

Local knowledge

In 1860, Robert O'Hara Burke and William John Wills
attempted to cross Australia from south to north.
Although they reached the northern coast, they starved
to death on the way back. If they had learnt how local
Aboriginal tribes survived in such harsh conditions, Burke
and Wills may well have lived – and discovered that the
Aboriginal peoples had explored it all before them!

Robert O'Hara Burke and
William John Wills

Long walk

In 1986, Michael Asher and Mariantonietta Peru set off to cross the Sahara Desert from west to east. They went on foot and with camels. The experience almost killed them: they nearly died of thirst, and hyenas would surround their camp at night. They were also arrested twice and were constantly afraid of being attacked by bandits. The journey took 271 days and covered around 7,500 kilometres, but they became the first people to complete such a trek.

Michael Asher

Mariantonietta Peru

39

10 At the bottom of the world

Not all deserts are hot. Antarctica is a desert! Antarctica is a world of rock and ice, howling gales and freezing temperatures, but less than 25 centimetres of snow fall there every year. What is it that attracts explorers to this frozen land?

Deadly

Oddly, it's the challenge of the terrible conditions that draws explorers. Some want to be the first to reach the very bottom of the world. Many never live to tell the tale. For example, all of Sir Robert Scott's 1911 team of explorers died of cold or starvation attempting to reach the South Pole. As recently as 2016, Colonel Wolsey died after trying to cross Antarctica on his own. He had to stop 48 kilometres short of his destination, suffering from severe exhaustion and lack of water.

Cool science

Imagine living somewhere as cold and unwelcoming as Antarctica. Conditions are so harsh that humans haven't tried to settle there – which is why scientists love it! It means they can study a habitat that hasn't been disturbed by humans.

Halley IV research station

You need a pretty special kind of place to stay in such conditions though. The Halley IV scientific station is like a hotel and laboratory in one. It's actually built on skis so it can be moved from place to place and its legs can be raised if the wind causes snow to build up. The base is used all year round and up to 70 scientists live and work there at a time.

Did you know?
Earth's coldest temperature was recorded in Antarctica, an unbelievable −97.8 degrees celsius. This makes the air too cold to breathe without killing you!

11 To infinity and beyond

While Antarctica is the toughest place to live on Earth, it's no match for space. There's no air to breathe and temperatures are either unbelievably hot or cold, depending whether you are in sunlight or in shade. Surviving in space needs skill, training and science, as travelling beyond our planet places explorers at extreme risk.

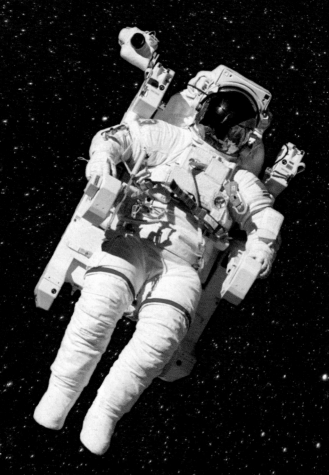

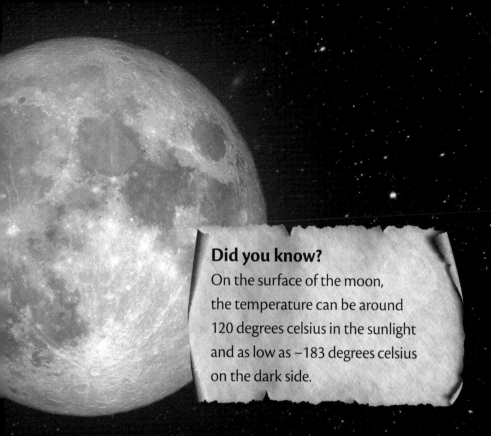

Did you know?
On the surface of the moon, the temperature can be around 120 degrees celsius in the sunlight and as low as –183 degrees celsius on the dark side.

Well dressed

If you found yourself floating in space without your spacesuit, you would be unconscious within 15 seconds and would be dead less than three minutes later.

An astronaut's spacesuit keeps their body at an even temperature, supplies oxygen to breathe and water to drink, as well as protecting them from space radiation. The visor on the helmet even works like sunglasses to protect the astronaut from the sun's glare.

Robots rule

Sending people out to explore space is dangerous and expensive. A safer way is to send machines instead. Space exploration is now done by satellites, rovers, telescopes and probes. It is hoped these mighty machines will unlock some of the great mysteries of space. Small remotely-controlled vehicles called rovers drive around our nearest planet, Mars, looking for signs of life. Space probes travel deep into our solar system and beyond, beaming back important data. Telescopes floating in space send back images that provide clues as to how big our universe is and how it began.

Excitingly, there are also hopes that one day people will be able to live and work on the moon, or even on Mars. Then we'll have whole new worlds to explore!

Did you know?
The first time astronauts travelled around the moon, scientists believed they had only a 50/50 chance of surviving.

12 Into the future

We have explored and discovered so much – is there anything left to find? The short answer to that is yes, there is *so* much we don't know about our planet. We haven't properly explored our highest mountains, our rainforests or our oceans. There's still so much to find.

New tech

An explorer's life has become much easier thanks to the latest technology. Drones allow you to see things you can't from the ground. Lasers can show what's hidden below vegetation or underground and sonars can show you what lies at the bottom of the sea.

Safe exploration

Of course, the biggest area to explore is the unlimited
space of the universe. Ironically, the further away from
home we search, the less we travel. The extreme distances
of space mean much of the research is done by scientists
studying data in laboratories, universities and even
from home. Making amazing discoveries no longer means
risking life and limb!

13 Great explorers

Ibn Battuta (born 1304 – died 1368)

Born in Morocco, Ibn Battuta spent around 29 years travelling 120,000 kilometres across Africa, India, South-East Asia and the Middle East. During his travels, he experienced storms, trekked from the top to the bottom of the Sahara, was shipwrecked, kidnapped, and robbers stole everything from him but his trousers.

Zheng He (born 1371 – died 1433)

The Chinese admiral was in charge of seven expeditions that were said to have ventured from China to the bottom tip of southern Africa. Taking over 200 ships in order to trade and collect interesting objects, Zheng He managed to bring back a giraffe from Kenya to present to the Chinese emperor.

Mary Kingsley (born 1862 – died 1900)

At a time when women in Britain had few rights, Mary Kingsley travelled from England and explored West and Central Africa. She met tribes that had never seen a European before and collected animals for the British Museum. She died of a disease called typhoid while volunteering as nurse during the Boer War in South Africa.

Matthew Henson (born 1866 – died 1955)

African-American Matthew Henson went from being an orphaned cabin boy to possibly being one of the first people to reach the North Pole. He was part of Robert Peary's polar expedition to the North Pole in 1906 and, although Peary got the credit for being first, it's thought Henson reached it before him.

Aloha Wanderwell (born 1906 – died 1966)

When a 16-year-old Canadian girl called Idris Welsh saw an advertisement to join a round-the-world expedition in 1922, she didn't hesitate to apply. She got the job, changed her name to Aloha Wanderwell and found fame and fortune. In an amazing and adventurous life, Aloha became

ALOHA WANDERWELL

The World's Most Widely Travelled Girl
1922 – 1930

the first woman to drive around the world, was made an honorary colonel in the Russian army, made friends with bandits, crash-landed in the Amazon rainforest, made documentary films, gave lectures and hung out with Hollywood film stars.

Helen Thayer (born 1937)

Even when she was a child, New Zealand explorer Helen Thayer was climbing mountains. Since then, she has walked across the Arctic to the North Pole on her own, walked across the Sahara and kayaked up the Amazon river. She has even lived with a pack of wolves for six months!

Sir Ranulph Fiennes (born 1944)

Described by the *Guinness Book of Records* as the world's greatest living explorer, Sir Ranulph Fiennes has climbed mountains (including Everest), trekked across both the Arctic and Antarctica, and led the team that discovered a lost city in the Yemen.

Exploring different places

Around the world

Under the sea

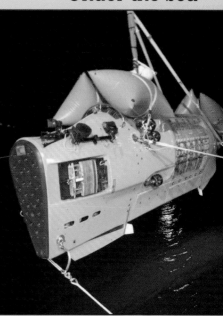

Rivers

Jungles

54

Mountains

Underground

Deserts

Space

 Ideas for reading

Written by Gill Matthews
Primary Literacy Consultant

Reading objectives:
- read books that are structured in different ways and read for a range of purposes
- retrieve, record and present information from non-fiction

Spoken language objectives:
- participate in discussions, presentations, performances, role play, improvisations and debates.

Curriculum links: Geography – Place knowledge

Interest words: actually, barely, exactly, unbearably

Resources: ICT

Build a context for reading

- Give children time to look closely at the front cover. Ask what kind of book they think this is and what it might be about.
- Read the blurb and explore children's understanding of extreme exploration. Establish what they know about exploration of the areas mentioned in the blurb. Ask why they think exploring these areas might be *extreme*.
- Ask where they will get more ideas about what is in the book. Turn to the contents page and give children time to read the entries.

Understand and apply reading strategies

- Read pp2–3 aloud to children. Check whether they have any questions as a result.
- Ask them to return to the contents page and choose a chapter to read. They can then formulate three questions that they would like to find answers to in that chapter.
- Give children time to read their chosen chapter. They can then feed back to the rest of the group on their reading and whether they found the answers to their questions.
- Ask children to share the most interesting fact that they have read.